CROCODILES

Can you say
snap, snap
like a crocodile?

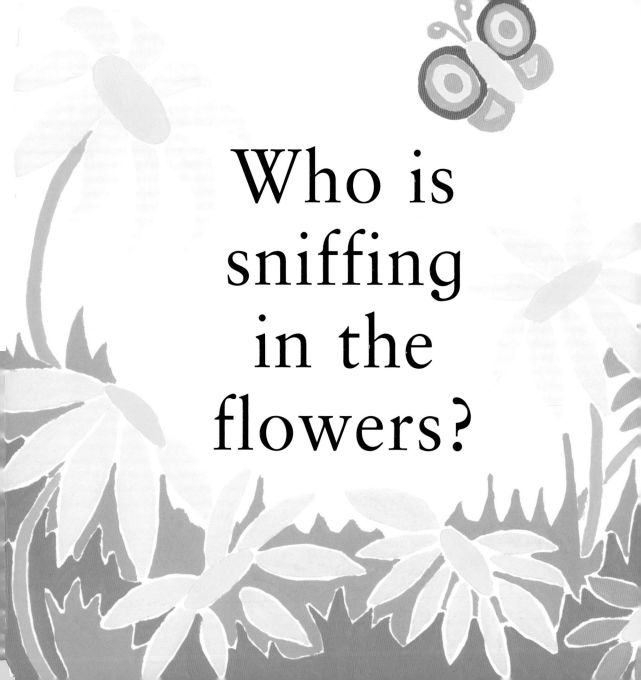

Who is
sniffing
in the
flowers?

DOG

Can you sniff
and bark like
a dog?

Who is sitting on the branch?

PARROTS

Can you squawk like a parrot?

Who is
snuffling
in the
orchard?

PIGS

Can you snuffle
and oink
like a pig?

Who is swimming in the ocean?